To Bart – to increase your menutia to include our favorite – John D.

Ann

by Leonore Fleischer

John Denver

NEW YORK   *Flash*   LONDON

CONTENTS

One: John Denver 7
Two: John's Television Career 31
Three: In Concert 39
Four: At Home in Colorado 49
Five: Denver and est 57
Six: Denver Talks About His Music and Others' 63
Seven: Denver vs. the Critics 71
Discography 76

Copyright © Flash Books, 1976
All rights reserved.

International Standard Book Number:
 0-8256-3909-3
Library of Congress Catalog Card Number:
 76-8065
Printed in the United States of America.

No part of this book may be reproduced or transmitted in any form or by any means, electronic or mechanical, including photocopying, without permission in writing from the publisher: Flash Books, A Division of Music Sales Corporation, 33 West 60th Street, New York 10023.

In Great Britain: Book Sales Ltd., 78 Newman Street, London W1, England.
In Canada: Gage Trade Publishing, P. O. Box 5000, 164 Commander Blvd., Agincourt, Ontario M1S 3C7.

Designed by Jon Goodchild
Front cover photograph by Bruce Ditchfield
Back cover photographs courtesy of RCA Records

JOHN DENVER

Colorado Magazine

ONE

If he were a flower, he would be a daisy. If he were a car, he would be a Chevy; if he were a single phrase he would be "Faarrr OUT!" If he were ice cream, he'd be vanilla, and if he were a color, he'd be green—the green of Colorado trees and of American money. But John Denver is not a flower, nor a car; he is not words nor flavor nor color. He is, rather, the living embodiment of the American Dream. For what is the American Dream if not a schizophrenic desire to get it *all* and still be known as a good guy, to be filthy rich and Mr. Clean, to be on top of everybody and still be loved by those on the bottom? And that's John Denver, RCA's greatest natural resource and ecology's most celebrated spokesman, a young man who has sold more than one hundred million records at this writing, and looks to sell a hundred million more.

"The music that I do is an effort to communicate the joy I have in living," Denver has said on more than one occasion, and it is this joy, this optimism, this romantic view from rose-colored granny glasses, that has made John Denver the world's largest-selling recording artist. He's top forty, he's easy listening, he's country and western, he's pop-rock; he styles himself as "contemporary," and his brown workboots leap across all musical barriers. In the 1975 *Billboard* year-end listings, Denver came in a prodigious Number One in no fewer than *four* categories—top singles artist, overall pop artist, easy listening artist and and country album. That's crossover with

something of a vengeance! Middle America, middle of the road—he's the quintessential clean hippie. You could bring him home to Mother, and he'd arrive in his own Learjet. Professing an affinity for his brother the eagle, he has defended the bighorn sheep and the grizzly bear with equal fervor, and breathes there any vanishing American species to whose defense he will not rise at the drop of a guitar chord? Aided by that great leveler, television, John Denver has parlayed a strong melodic sensitivity and a love of the outdoors into a show-biz shtick that reportedly grossed between ten and fourteen million dollars in 1974 alone.

His detractors have labeled Denver as the "Mickey Mouse of Rock Music" or the "Pollyanna of Pop." *Time* magazine profiled him as the "Tom Sawyer of Rock," and he's also been tagged as Mary Poppins, Peter Pan, Lawrence Welk, "packaged nature," "Glen Campbell with a coat hanger in his mouth," and the "Rod McKuen of endangered species." Frank Sinatra remarked that Denver looked like a "butch Barbie Doll," an unkind cut with more than a single barb of truth in it. For every fan who admires John Denver as gentle, cheery, wholesome, homespun, simple, hopeful and sincere, there's a critic to snarl at him as bland, saccharine, escapist, super-straight, cornball, hokey and pseudo-country. Is his music a celebration of life or is it watered down for mass consumption? Is the best thing about Denver that he's inoffensive, or is that the worst thing about him? Peter Fornatale summed up his appeal several years ago when he wrote, "John has the elusive ability to make you feel good." And everybody wants to feel good, which is why John Denver is a millionaire.

The facts of Denver's life are public domain. He has recited them so often and so frequently in the very same words that Sinatra's Barbie Doll image is reinforced. It's as though there were a string in Denver's side; pull it and you get one of fourteen or fifteen public statements: "The music flows through me," or "I live the perfect life," or "I changed my name because they told me it wouldn't fit on a record label," or "My grandmother gave me a 1910 Gibson guitar when I was a kid," or "I wrote 'Annie's Song' in a ski-lift in Aspen, and it's a ten minute ride." Recently, on Merv Griffin's show, John was the only guest and he told the story of his life with a charming frankness and a wealth of detail, in *almost exactly the same phrases he'd used in interviews given four or five years ago.* If nothing else, that's consistency!

The composer of "Leaving, on a Jet Plane," "Rocky Mountain High," "Sunshine on My Shoulders," "Sweet Surrender," "Annie's Song," and more than fifty others was born on December 31, 1943, a New Year's Eve baby, in Roswell, New Mexico. His parents were Henry John and Erma Deutschendorf, and the boy was named Henry John Deutschendorf, Jr. His father, Henry John Sr., a lieutenant colonel in the Air Force, was only temporarily stationed in Roswell, and the family was soon on the move. They lived in Arizona, Alabama, Ohio, Texas and Japan, and Denver's childhood was a lonely one.

"I wanted to be accepted and I wanted to be liked," Denver has told interviewers over the years. "I never had any close friends because just when I would acquire them, Dad would yank me out of school because we were moving again, to Alabama or Arkansas or some such place. I was in the seventh and eighth grades in Tucson, Arizona, and in the ninth grade in Montgomery, Alabama, where I was thirteen years old and started school a week after everybody else had been there, not knowing a soul. A very insecure, unsure, self-conscious thirteen-year-old going from Arizona to Alabama to Texas, three completely different environments. Well, I think everybody wants people to like them, to be able to communicate with people. I always signed up for chorus instead of study hall."

John's grandmother had given him a 1910 Gibson guitar when he was ten, and had taught him to play it, both the six-string and the twelve-string. In Montgomery, feeling "very much out of touch and out of place," John used his musical ability to make friends. "One day I brought my guitar to a chorus class and sang a couple of songs that I had written and all of a sudden people were saying hello to me in halls and

I was getting invited to parties and stuff. It helped me to break into the circle of people who knew each other and had grown up together in Montgomery, and I made friends. And the same thing happened when we moved to Texas. Music is what opened the door for me."

Music had begun to be more to John than just a key to the locked door of popularity. Elvis Presley was one source of renewed inspiration. "All of a sudden, there was music on the radio that appealed to me. I started playing again and just got deeper and deeper into it." John formed a trio and played and sang at proms and parties. And he changed his mind about what direction he wanted his life to take.

Henry John Deutschendorf, Sr., held three world aviation records, and John had planned to follow in his father's wingbeats—to make his career in the skies. But now, his thoughts turned to becoming a singer.

"What I didn't want was to go on to college, and that's what really got my parents upset. First of all, they thought my ideas of being an entertainer were childish fantasy, and they didn't see it as an honest or stable way to make a living! They'd always dreamed of my going to college. It never occurred to them that I might not want to go. And I just didn't see where college fit into my plans at all. I was sixteen then.

"As you can imagine, all sorts of conflicts developed. I mean there was a point where *all* we'd do was argue. As time went by, my parents became angrier than ever and I became more and more frustrated. I finally decided there was only one solution—I'd run away!

"I made my move one night after everyone had gone to bed. I left a note saying, 'Goodbye, I've gone to become a star.' I packed up my guitar, some clothes and what little money I had and hopped aboard a bus going to California. Of course, I hadn't given any thought to what I would do once I got there.

"I arrived in Los Angeles tired, hungry and very scared. I was too petrified to check into a hotel, so I wandered the streets trying to think. Hollywood was not at all the place I imagined it would be. It was so *big*, and so *busy*! Everyone seemed to be rushing somewhere and no one at all paid the slightest attention to me. I finally decided that I had to get some rest and tried the first small, quiet-looking hotel I could find. The proprietor eyed me suspiciously and asked how old I was.

" 'Eighteen,' I lied. Now, I know he didn't believe me for one second, but he did give me a room. I was so relieved, I just conked out for fourteen hours. Reality hit me very hard the next morning, when I had to pay for my room. Between that and breakfast, I was flat broke already!"

Scared, John called his folks to get the telephone number of a family friend in L.A. He went to stay with them and "Dad came out and got me and we drove home together and talked a little bit but I don't know that anything was really solved then. So we got back together."

John was graduated from Arlington Heights High School in Fort Worth, Texas. "When I finished high school, I didn't know what to do with my life. The only acceptable thing I seemed to enjoy was drawing and designing, so I said, well, I'll major in architecture. We found a good school, Texas Tech. That was legitimate. If I grew up to be an architect, my dad would be pretty happy with me. My folks paid my tuition, room and board, and I earned the rest.

"I was part of a rhythm and blues band, sang with a trio, then went solo. People were willing to listen to me, and singing for them was the only way I got high. I was learning from Joan Baez and Tom Paxton and the Chad Mitchell Trio and Peter, Paul and Mary and the New Christy Minstrels. I was just eating that up. I loved all of that music. That was the kind of music I had been singing and now it had a label. People called it folk music. So I was doing all of that music and I was going to school and enjoying the architecture, but nothing was happening in Texas with the exception of the music and nothing else really worked for me. The one thing I really decided to do as good as I could and learn and grow with was the music that I did.

"By the time I had been there two and a half years, I was spending more hours with

my music than in classes. My grades were suffering and there was little that seemed relevant to my life. And it got to the point again that things got hard with my parents. Finally, I built up enough courage to leave, and halfway through my junior year at the semester break I left. Everybody—and I mean *everybody*—said that I was making the biggest mistake in my life. My parents, my best friends, everybody said I was making a mistake. Not one said, 'Go ahead, John, and good luck to you.' They said, 'John, you'll be sorry.' Also, I found out they'd been betting on how long I was gonna last. My friends in the architecture department had been betting on whether I was gonna last through the semester.

"And then I'd gone home to my folks and all they did was give me shit about my grades and there was really no interest in finding out what was going on for me in my life and so finally I left. That last week before I left, I didn't sleep at all. Man, it was a very scary thing to step off that way! But I got into the car, the old brown goose, a '53 Chevrolet loaded down with three guitars, my architectural equipment, everything I owned, and headed out to California with $125. I left early, about seven o'clock on a Thursday morning, and by noon I was happier than I had ever been in my whole life."

Writing home, John told his folks that he had left to make a career in music. "And they did what was probably one of the best things they ever did for me, and I think the greatest thing any parents could do for their children: they gave me the space to go. They sent me $200 and they said, 'We don't approve of this. We would prefer that you stay in college and we think you're gonna go slouch around and when you're tired of playing around like that, then let us know and we'll help you go on from there with your education.' I think they had the feeling that music was something you really like to listen to and it was nice that I had a talent—played guitar and sang in the choir and stuff like that—but entertainment wasn't something you did for a living."

That was 1964. Arriving in Los Angeles again, John managed to get a job as a draftsman and began making the rounds of the folkie haunts looking for work as a singer. "I began singing everywhere I could until—hopefully—somebody would hire me. I went to all the hootenannies and they were going on all over everywhere in L.A. The second year I was there I went to Leadbetter's, which was owned by Randy Sparks. [Sparks was the man behind the New Christy Minstrels and the Back Porch Majority.] I sang and he came back after the show and said he'd really like my voice and would like to talk to me about working there.

"It *totally* flipped me out and it came from two things," Denver told Chet Flippo in his *Rolling Stone* cover interview. "Randy liked me and saw potential and also Leadbetter's was put together as a place for people to get their acts together so they could fit into the New Christy Minstrels. The Back Porch Majority was kind of a farm club for the Christy Minstrels and when the Majority got good enough to go out on the road there was then a farm club for *them*. Somehow, within that framework, Randy had me working as a single. Someone somewhere has a tape of the first week I worked there and I think you would be amazed at how—in a sense—how *bad* I was, but, see, I went from being just really *terrible* to being only pretty bad in about five days.

"That first weekend I started getting encores and then I was extended to 26 weeks there, and started getting jobs around the country. I signed a contract, which I couldn't legally do because I was only 20 but I wasn't gonna let not being 21 get in the way, so I lied and signed.

"But then Randy was getting tired of me, and on a trip I auditioned at a club in Phoenix called the Lumbermill and they hired me. I went back to L.A. and got a call that Chad Mitchell was leaving the Trio and had given them six months to find somebody to replace him and wow! this was far out! Here was a chance to audition for somebody I had listened to in college. They were interested in the audition tape I sent and they flew me to New York. I guess they had gotten 250 or 300 other tapes and I had had a cold and I was trying to sing like Chad. So I got to New York and at the first audition I tried to sing like Chad and just did *terrible* and they sent me over to Joe Frazier's house [a Trio member] on the West Side and I learned two songs. And about an hour and a half later we went back to Milt Okun's office with Joe singing with me and it was a whole different thing.

"They sent me back to Phoenix and said don't call us, we'll call you. So I sat around waiting for the phone call. I mean, I didn't leave the motel at all except to go to the Lumbermill to work at night. A couple of days later the call came and they *had* picked me. So we rehearsed for six days and then opened at the Cellar Door in Washington, D.C. So that started the Chad Mitchell thing." Henry John Deutschendorf, Jr., by now self-christened John Denver at the urging of Randy Sparks, remained with the Mitchell Trio for three years.

"At first, I wasn't too happy about changing my last name. Everyone told me that my name was too hard for people to remember and pronounce and that it wouldn't fit on marquees and record labels. Some of the last names suggested to me were things like Summerville and Dutch. Those names didn't do very much for me. I chose the name of Denver because I love the city and I felt comfortable with it. But I'm proud of both names. John Deutschendorf could be an architect or he might be a teacher, but John Denver would never have a job where he had to work nine to five. He needs to be free!"

In his first year with the Mitchell Trio, Denver wrote the song that was to become the means to his first fame, as a composer rather than a singer. It was "Leaving, on a Jet Plane."

One night in 1966, the Mitchell Trio was playing Washington, D.C. "We were always being invited to parties," Denver recalled. "I was never the type to play around on the road, and time after time I'd be the only guy at the party without a girl. This time I decided I'd had it with that. When the others left for the party at eight, I got a pound of salami and a six-pack of beer and my guitar and locked myself in my room. When they came back around midnight, I had eaten the salami, drunk all the beer, and written 'Jet Plane.' It was a pretty productive night.

"You go to school and you find someone you care about and then Christmas vacation comes up or whatever and you go home to your family and they usually fly and stuff; kids are going to school out of state generally. Everyone at one time or another has to say goodbye to someone that they care about and that's really all the song is about. And it just came at a time when a lot of people could identify with it and it freaked me out. It really was unexpected.

"I guess there were two factors in my writing the song. First, I really enjoy meeting people. Frequently while traveling, doing one-night stands, I'd meet someone and it clicked, and I'd wish I had time to get to know them better. There was that, and then a personal factor, a girl I cared about." Girl or no girl, Denver is quoted again and again as saying, "I wrote 'Leaving, on a Jet Plane' as much out of a desire to have someone to sing it to as to sing it to someone."

Either way, the successful folk trio of Peter, Paul and Mary recorded it in 1967, on their album *1700*, but it wasn't until the group released the song as a single in 1969 that it became a smash hit, climbing up the charts to first place and staying there for many weeks. By that time the Mitchell Trio had broken up, and John was scuffling to make a living as a solo on the coffeehouse and folk club circuit.

At the time Denver had joined the Trio, folk music was on the way out, as rock and roll bands became more popular. It was the raucous time of the Beatles and the Stones, the psychedelic San Francisco sound; Dylan had gone electric, and the acoustical guitar was forced to make way for the amplified instruments. "It was a downhill trip when I joined," Denver remembers. By the beginning of 1968, John Denver was the only "original" member of the Trio. It, and he, were more than $40,000 in debt. "I believed in the Trio and what we were doing. We didn't have a big following. We didn't pack the places, but the people came in and loved what we did. There was some substance to our show. I believed in that and wanted to continue in that line. I decided that I'd stay with it as long as everybody else wanted to, but as soon as one guy wanted to quit, I'd be through with groups."

By November 22, 1968, when the Mitchell Trio played its last gig, John Denver was a married man. He had met Ann Martell when the Trio did a concert at Gustavus Adolphus College in St. Peter, Minnesota. After the concert, the entertainers stayed to see a fraternity-sorority fund-raising revue.

"Annie was in one of the skits," recalls Denver. "She was the girl who came out between the acts, carrying signs that said, *Act One, Act Two, Applause*. She was wearing jeans and penny loafers and no socks and a big, baggy plaid wool shirt. She had long dark hair and I fell in love with her. I really did." They were married in June, 1967, and moved to Chicago, which Denver hated.

"When the trio broke up, I had no work, no money, nothing. I had absolutely nothing except Annie and me and an apartment in Chicago that we couldn't afford and all those debts. It was down to $11,000. Somebody hired me for a week at a club just outside Aspen. I did very well for the week and they kept me on for January. I had some friends at the Cellar Door in Washington and they gave me a chance to come in and work as a second act there. Then, I got three weeks of work on the campus coffee-house circuit. That was about two months of work. It was able to keep Annie and me going and pay a little money on the debt and give me some time to get some dates going."

Actually, two factors came into play at this hand-to-mouth period in Denver's life, two factors which were to solidify his position as an entertainer and set his feet firmly on the rungs of Fortune's slippery golden ladder. The first was "Leaving, on a Jet Plane," which, as a reissued Peter, Paul and Mary single, was climbing pellmell to the top. John was gaining new and larger audiences through being billed as the composer of "Jet Plane"; it was bringing him better gigs and more money. The second factor was Jerry Weintraub.

"I took Denver from a $75-a-night

acoustical guitarist and singer to the biggest star in the world," says Weintraub grandly. "It's the proudest thing in my life." In the teeming ocean of artist management, Weintraub is Monstro the Whale. At 38, he has more energy than ever, and balances movies, television, concerts and recordings with the skill of a music-hall juggler. He produced Robert Altman's *Nashville*, and his other credits include: *Sinatra, the Main Event at Madison Square Garden*, Sinatra and Denver on the same bill at Harrah's, Lake Tahoe, the national concert tours of Elvis Presley, Led Zeppelin and the Moody Blues, Geraldo Rivera's "Good Night, America," and John Denver's Emmy-winning TV special, to name but a handful. When Weintraub and Denver met, the former had just turned 30, the latter 27.

John Denver, out on his own after the Trio broke up, walked into Weintraub's New York office and asked him to be his manager. "We talked," remembers Weintraub. "I looked at him, he looked at me and we made a deal even though I'd never heard him sing or seen his show. I didn't even see him work for a year after I'd signed him, but I had a hunch and it paid off." But Weintraub did eventually see Denver work. "He'll be the biggest star in America some day," he announced prophetically in 1970, when Denver was headlining at the Troubadour in West Hollywood. "He'll be able to appeal to both young people and to an older audience that usually refuses to listen to contemporary acts. They'll listen to John—and let him into their homes on television—because they feel comfortable with him. And John will reach out for them. A lot of younger acts just want to carve out a special little audience. But John wants to reach everybody with his music." These were the words that Weintraub was to back up with a type of management that made them come true ten times over, but he started his management of Denver modestly enough. In a sort of market-research technique, he sent John back out to the boondocks to do his solo act. "John wasn't selling any records and being out there was the only way he could get his music across. It was a grassroots campaign. We went to the people first, and the people said 'You're great!' John was selling out in Texas, Iowa, St. Louis and Kansas City before anybody in New York City knew who he was."

Today, Weintraub drives a Rolls-Royce that was a Christmas present from John Denver in 1975; on the wall of his office is the framed Xerox of a check made out to Denver by RCA for two and a half million dollars, representing six months of record royalties, six particularly fat months.

"I'm a student of Mike Todd, Cecil B. DeMille and P.T. Barnum," claims Weintraub as he lights another cigar. "I do things bigger than anyone. I'm talented, creative, lucky and the best at what I do." If the success of John Denver is the measure of that boast, then who can deny it?

In 1969 an audition with RCA Records was arranged for Denver by Milt Okun (who became the producer on all of Denver's albums and a man who John feels was the most influential on his music; "Milt has been my guiding light," Denver has been quoted as saying. "He's given me direction without being restrictive"). After only one audition, RCA signed the young man to a two-year contract. October of the same year saw the release of John Denver's first solo album, *Rhymes & Reasons*. It was not a distinguished album; of the twelve musical cuts, only three were of Denver's own composition—"Leaving, on a Jet Plane," "Daydreams" and the title song, "Rhymes & Reasons," an early Denver plea for grown-ups to find the innocence of children and flowers. "Like the music of the mountains and the colors of the rainbow, they're a promise of the future and a blessing for today," go the lyrics. Marring the album was a gross rendition of Lennon-McCartney's delicious "When I'm Sixty-Four," sung loudly and with excruciating archness, a thoroughly amateur effort. A pair of feeble attempts at Mitchell Trio-type political satire were two cuts: "The Ballad of Spiro Agnew" and "The Ballad of Richard Nixon," in which the good deeds of these worthies were recorded by several seconds of silence. Meanwhile, "Leaving, on a Jet Plane" was being waxed by nearly everybody—Liza Minnelli, Claudine Longet, Floyd Cramer, Spanky and Our Gang, Eddy

Arnold, and Josh White, Jr. It was even used for a while on United Airlines' television commercials.

Denver's second album, *Take Me to Tomorrow*, was released in the spring of 1970. It contained a much larger share of original Denver material than the first one; this time, six out of the eleven cuts were of John's composition: "Take Me to Tomorrow," "Isabel," "Follow Me," "Aspenglow," "Anthem—Revelation" and "Sticky Summer Weather." Denver had originally conceived of his first two albums as a unit, a concert, in fact. *Rhymes & Reasons*, with its lighter material, made up the first half—the "get-acquainted" half—of the concert, while *Take Me to Tomorrow* contained the "heavier" music, among which were two Tom Paxton songs, the satirical "Forest Lawn" and the antiwar "Jimmy Newman." As a matter of record, Denver pointed proudly to his inclusion of "Jimmy Newman" in all his concerts; he was, then, being queried publicly about his apparent lack of involvement in the antiwar efforts that were engaging the young people of America.

"If someone asked me what I am about," said Denver, "I'd say come listen to my concert. My best autobiography is the music I sing." He considered the diptych of *Rhymes & Reasons* and *Take Me to Tomorrow* as his musical autobiography.

The only song resembling a hit that came off the second album was "Follow Me," which he wrote for his wife Annie. "When we were first married, I couldn't afford to take her with me on tour with the Mitchell Trio. At times she couldn't understand why I had to leave and I couldn't blame her for feeling that way." When he wrote "Follow Me," John had been on the road for two and a half months. "I wrote the chorus somewhere in Iowa," he told Christopher Wren of the New York *Times*, "but I couldn't do anything with it. Then one afternoon in Washington, D.C., I wrote the rest of it. Paul Stookey [late of Peter, Paul and Mary] told me once that you're not so much the writer of a song as you are the instrument of what wants to be written." Both Mary Travers and June Carter Cash recorded "Follow Me," and it was a larger hit for them than for Denver.

In "Aspenglow," John Denver recorded his first "Colorado" song. After the Mitchell Trio had broken up, John went out to play small gigs in college towns and resorts, and the Leather Jug in Aspen was probably his most successful stint then. "I'd had a lot of beautiful experiences there. The whole stay had given me a tremendous lift when I badly needed one. The local people were so involved in that friendly way of life, and when I finally sat down to think about it, I wrote the song in about fifteen minutes. I tried to capture something of the spirit of the people there and the way they treated me. The friendliest people in the world, I think, are skiers."

In the fall of 1970, RCA released *Whose Garden Was This*, the title song of which was not written by John Denver but by Tom Paxton. "When I first heard Tom's song 'Whose Garden Was This' I started thinking about all the things that change as we grow older," wrote Denver in the liner

notes. "Things that we lose or forget, or that somehow pass us by. These songs are a reflection of those thoughts—having to do with today's memories and, perhaps, tomorrow's."

Whose Garden Was This was more laid back than the first two albums. John did not consider himself a good enough songwriter to fill an album with his own music exclusively. "My songs simply aren't good enough to fill a whole album time after time. I know that, but I want people to have a full album when they go to a record shop, and I like singing good songs, whether I wrote them or not.

"I've never been able to write songs about people. I consider people like John Prine and John Stewart truly American songwriters. They're able to write about people in a particular segment of society. I've never been able to write songs like 'Angel from Montgomery' [Prine], 'Cannons in the Rain' [Stewart], or 'Amsterdam' [Jacques Brel, who Denver once said he considered the foremost living composer]. That's why I record their songs rather than try to write something similar."

If you don't count an adaptation of sorts of "Jingle Bells," there are but three original Denver songs on *Garden*: "Sail Away Home," overlong and overdramatic; "I Wish I Could Have Been There," another Woodstock anthem; and "Sweet, Sweet Life," with which he capped the Lennon-McCartney "Golden Slumbers." Denver did nothing for "Eleanor Rigby" but make it monotonous, sang a plaintive Jerry Jeff Walker song, "Mr. Bojangles," in a manner that didn't give Harry Nilsson anything to worry about, and rendered "The Night They Drove Old Dixie Down" in a nasal tenor without either the muscularity of the Band or the tenderness of Baez. It is far from being a class-A album, either in conception or in execution.

As though in rebuttal to the undistinguished third album, John's fourth album, released in 1971, contained treasure, pure gold, and John's first big hit (excluding "Jet Plane," which was a hit in other versions than his own). *Poems, Prayers & Promises* included the beautiful "Take Me Home, Country Roads." This song, released as a single, went up to the top of the record charts and turned the album into a gold one. Peter Fornatale was to write later, " 'Take Me Home, Country Roads' crossed all audience lines and broke down all the artificial media categories. Someday, people might just point to it as the song that launched the new middle-of-the-road consciousness of the seventies." The song was the result of a collaboration between John and two of his friends, Bill Danoff and Taffy Nivert. Bill and Taffy, who billed themselves as Fat City, were working at the Cellar Door in Washington, D.C., with Denver. They had written a song for John, "I Guess He'd Rather Be in Colorado," which also appears on the *Poems, Prayers & Promises* album.

"After opening night at the Cellar Door we were gonna go back to their house and jam and we were in a car accident and my thumb was broken," John told *Rolling Stone*. "I went to the hospital to have a splint put on it and by then I was *wired*— you know, after a car wreck. So we went over to their house and in the early hours of the morning they showed me this chorus and part of the verse to a song they were

writing called 'Country Roads.' And I flipped over that song.

"They'd had it for a month and hadn't been able to do anything with what they had. That morning we finished writing that song and I said, we've got to record this on the next album, which was *Poems, Prayers & Promises*. Now here's the point I was trying to make about Jerry [Weintraub]. He heard it and said, 'Ah ha! Finally, a record worth working for.' He got onto it and by the end of March it had gotten up to about fifty on the charts—the first record we ever had on the charts—and RCA wanted to pull it back and release something else. Jerry and I both screamed. Also, the initial copies that were sent out were distorted and I raised a fit about that and got some help from RCA in getting it taken care of. But, see, I *knew* we had a good record and I was making an effort at being successful. Top 40 successful. Jerry and I kept at it and it went on to be a Number One record.

"It *really* changed the whole situation. I had a record on the charts and all of a sudden it's not John Denver, the writer of 'Leaving, on a Jet Plane,' but it's John Denver who sings the song that you hear on the radio. So a whole thing changed. All of this time, I was growing, learning more about myself, noticing what music was coming out of me and where it came from and how it worked and what it had to do with and so I was able to cut away a lot of the nonsense and bullshit that starts getting in. Like one of the things that I got through very quickly was: Well, now that you've had a hit, how are you going to follow that? What have you written since 'Jet Plane'? What have you written since 'Country Roads'? I finally got to a stage where I realized that I had never tried to write a hit record. And I haven't yet. I am the most unprolific songwriter that I know. I've gone periods of six months without writing a song."

Unknown to anybody at that time, there was another Number One cut on the *Poems, Prayers & Promises* album, "Sunshine on My Shoulders." But it would be a long time—from the spring of 1971 to the fall of 1973—before the song would hit big, and it was a television show that would bring it about.

Aside from everything else on the album, the title song got some airplay as well, particularly after the album itself went gold. "The best song I've ever written is 'Poems, Prayers & Promises,' " Denver has told everybody. "That song is my best statement. I couldn't have said in a more concise manner exactly where I stand in my life today. I feel good about that way of life, feel good about that song and about that viewpoint and I don't want that to change and I'm really trying to be wary of not getting carried away with all this [success]." It is a frankly sentimental song about the joys of loving . . . "of poems and prayers and promises, and things that we believe in, how sweet it is to love someone, how right it is to care. How long it's been since yesterday, and what about tomorrow? And what about our dreams and all the memories we shared?"

With a Number One hit, John and Annie were able to move to Aspen, to the Colorado of their dreams. High in the Rockies, they built their house of glass and wood, and John began to watch the stars and the flight of eagles. This led to his fifth album, *Aerie*, a celebration of the mountain tops and the glorious birds of prey who make their nests high thereon. *Aerie* gave John his first expression of the eagle-and-the-hawk theme, the embodiment of flying free. "Come dance with the west wind and touch on the mountain tops, sail o'er the canyons and up to the stars. And reach for the heavens and hope for the future, and all that we can be and not what we are."

By now, John's themes of free mountain living and fresh country air were becoming familiar to millions of radio listeners and record buyers. By spring, 1972, when *Aerie* came onto the market, John Denver was completely identified with "Take Me Home, Country Roads" and a boyish personality projection. Only one thing was missing—mass exposure via the tube. Which was a situation that was about to change drastically.

Only four of the songs of *Aerie* were Denver compositions, if you don't count a sixty-second bank commercial that he

included for funsies. "Starwood in Aspen" tells of Denver's "sweet Rocky Mountain paradise," where his friends are the snow-covered hills. "It's a long way from L.A. to Denver, to Starwood in Aspen . . . ," he croons, giving one the picture of a young man running free on the mountain tops. Actually, Starwood—where John and Annie live—is one of Aspen's most expensive and exclusive residential communities, high above the town of Aspen. Homes built there are worth hundreds of thousands of dollars, and the roads to those castles are protected from the peasantry by a guard in a wooden bunker. Ah, well, it's a pretty song, anyway.

"All of My Memories," which Denver has described as "the prettiest song I've ever written," is again a celebration of moving to Colorado after a life spent on the road. "All my memories lay in the life of the highway . . . ." With "Tools" and "The Eagle and the Hawk," these made up the Denver-written portion of the album. The other songs included John Prine's satirical "Blow Up Your TV (Spanish Pipe Dream)," the Steve Goodman-John Denver "City of New Orleans" (which Arlo Guthrie recorded later and better), and "Casey's Last Ride," a Kristofferson tune. Denver had been hoping that "Everyday" (by Charles Hardin) would be released as a single to follow up his giant hit, "Take Me Home, Country Roads." "Everyday" was an old Bobby Vee hit back in 1960, and John felt that it had the potential of hitting in the top 40, middle of the road, country and western stations across the board. But instead RCA released "Friends with You," by Taffy Nivert and Bill Danoff, as the album's single. Actually, *Aerie* was a slow starter as an album, and, while it did eventually go gold, it was the success of Denver's next album *Rocky Mountain High* and his burgeoning TV career that pushed *Aerie*'s sales.

"He was born in the summer of his 27th year / Comin' home to a place he'd never been before / He left yesterday behind him, you might say he was born again / You might say he found a key for every door. . . ." Thus begins the most celebrated song on the most celebrated album of Denver's celebrated career, *Rocky*

Mountain High. It was Denver's first platinum album, the first of five. (A gold album is one that has sold a million dollars' worth of units; a platinum album has sold a million hot *units*.)

" 'Rocky Mountain High' took about nine months to write," John told Chet Flippo in *Rolling Stone*. "I had the chorus to it that I had gotten from a camping trip at William Lake, about 26 miles from Aspen. I was telling these guys about this meteor shower. I said, you guys are gonna see some shooting stars tonight and you're not gonna believe it. So it's gettin' dark and I noticed there was no moon that night, and we were up at about 11,000 feet and there're so many stars and the sky gets to be so deep and clear that you have a little pool of shadows from the starlight. And then these guys were saying, all right, shooting stars. . . . And then pretty soon there were balls of fire going across. It goes all the way across the sky, you can see the smoke, you can see it and you can *hear* it.

"It's great, it's so far out, and I was saying, Rocky Mountain high, I've seen a ray of fire in the sky, and the shadow of the starlight, look at that. And then it took me a while to write that song, to put the story around that song, which is totally autobiographical."

A good song about "coming home," about finding oneself and being spiritually reborn, could hardly fail in today's inner-directed society. And "Rocky Mountain High" is a *very* good song; it touches people closely, as Denver has said again and again he wants to do.

Released in October of 1972, when Denver was not yet twenty-nine years old, it catapulted him to the number one position in the record world, the top song and the top album on the charts. It was even a well-reviewed album; critics had been finding fault with the lush arrangements and heavy strings on the earlier albums. Now Bud Scoppa praised it in *Rolling Stone*, saying, ". . . it's a crisp, muscular album with compelling singing and some of the most powerful acoustic guitar-dominated arrangements I've heard on record." Scoppa then voiced a general criticism about

Denver's good-little-boy musical image. "More than anything, Denver needed some hard edges—some arrogance, meanness, smelliness, some unspeakable aberration—anything that would dirty up his act." But with the advent of Denver's television success, this would become a forlorn hope; the clean would become squeaky-clean, and the shine would become polish. As for hard edges—forget it!

But *Rocky Mountain High* was not merely a one-song album. Another huge hit was to come from it—"Goodbye Again," written for Annie Denver, and the third song in the "goodbye trilogy" that began with "Leaving, on a Jet Plane" and continued with "Follow Me." "Annie, my wife, she doesn't like to travel, so I have to keep leaving her behind all the time. I don't like that very much. I guess that's one of the things I was trying to say in 'Goodbye Again.' People say I write a lot of songs about the road and saying goodbye, so I guess home really means a lot to me. It's a funny thing about songs. 'Jet Plane,' 'Follow Me,' and 'Goodbye Again' are basically the same song. They're all about leaving someone you love for whatever reason. I think each song is a little bit older. I'd like to think it's a sign that I'm maturing, but I don't know if I'm the one to judge that. I don't think I'm a very mature person sometimes. But I do think the songs are maturing."

"Every song on the album relates to the environment in some way," explained Denver. He chose the Lennon-McCartney favorite, "Mother Nature's Son," and John Prine's "Paradise," and a country-style ballad called "Darcy Farrow," by Steve Gillette and Tom Campbell. But, for the first time, a Denver album was dominated by Denver songs—four songs and a six-part suite, "Season Suite." He had also been refining his concerts, eliminating many of the minor songs and developing and perfecting his persona of cleanliness. After the *Rocky Mountain High* album went to the top, he would begin every concert with it, projecting on a three-part giant screen beautiful color footage of Colorado and home movies of himself, Annie, his friends and his pets, all romping in the clean snows and green woods of the Rockies.

"Nobody in the world has recorded 'Rocky Mountain High,'" he bragged. "It's a hard song to sing and a hard song to play." But that scarcely seems the reason. Who would dare to record another man's theme song, a personal statement so totally identified with him as to be inseparable from the Denver personality?

"Andromeda Quasar lives!" announced John Denver on the dedication to *Rocky Mountain High*. *Farewell Andromeda* was the title of his next album. In between the two, John had taken est training (Erhard Seminar Training), a new and fashionable approach to gaining control of one's own life. Did Andromeda have anything to do with est? Quasar? Was the album named after John's cat, or was the cat herself named for something more significant? "Andromeda is a constellation and a galaxy, and a quasar is a beam of light from the far reaches of space . . . I think that's all I wanted to say about it. It's a personal creation of mine and it probably wouldn't mean anything to someone else." Astronomy was a new hobby of John's; the Starwood house boasted a glass-enclosed tower with a telescope through which John had been watching the stars.

John went on record as considering *Farewell Andromeda* "twice as good as *Rocky Mountain High*. That was a giant record. I don't know if the new one will have as much success. But it's okay with me if it doesn't. This album is exactly what I wanted to do. It reflects me . . . who I am, what I feel. One side probes the depths of country music before the likes of John Prine were discovered. The second side is my philosophy of life, as close as I think I can get to it on record."

The "country" side began with a twangy number that became the album's big hit, "I'd Rather Be a Cowboy," about a free spirit who'd rather ride the range than wear a lady's chains. It was the only Denver song on that side, the others being supplied by John Prine, Hoyt Axton, Bryan Bowers, and Nivert and Danoff.("Please, Daddy," a satirical country and western number that had a little child pleading with poppa not to get drunk this Christmas, Denver predicted would be bigger than "Rudolph, the Red Nosed Reindeer." It wasn't.)

The "philosophy" side of the album featured four Denver songs out of the six on the side: "Rocky Mountain Suite (Cold Nights in Canada)," "Whiskey Basin Blues," "Zachary and Jennifer" (a song to future children), and the other hit song of the album, "Farewell Andromeda (Welcome to My Morning)." "Welcome to my morning, welcome to my day / Oh, yes, I'm the one responsible / I made it just this way / To make myself some pictures and see what they might bring / I think I made it perfectly / I wouldn't change a thing." That song was truly the quintessence of the Denver optimism, fortified by est.

Although there was still a heavy use of strings overpowering some of the cuts on this seventh album of Denver's, there was often a simplicity, too, missing from many of the arrangements on earlier albums, missing and, frankly, missed. Banjo, dulcimer, acoustic guitar, flute, harmonica and woodwinds often combined to present a quiet country feeling without the overpowering lusciousness that critics continually complained of, and which made so many of Denver's numbers sound alike. Strings spoiled, for example, parts of "I'd Rather Be a Cowboy," but worked very well on "Whiskey Basin Blues." Dedicated to "All of you from Werner [Erhard] and EST and me," *Farewell*

Andromeda shipped gold. Along with *Rocky Mountain High*, it stayed in the top ten for months.

"*Farewell Andromeda* was written out of a thing called est," John told an interviewer, just after *Poems, Prayers & Promises* and *John Denver's Greatest Hits* both went platinum in the same week. "It's a situation that allows people to get in touch with each other and life. As I said before, I'm interested in what works. The song came out of the est experience. If there's any time in your life when you feel empty, or just don't feel good, maybe you should take the time to look into it. One of the experiences of life is listening to yourself, finding yourself, getting in touch with where you are in the universe."

In November 1973, just in time for Denver's thirtieth birthday, RCA released *John Denver's Greatest Hits*, which put together a retrospective of the biggest of the moneymakers. Interestingly enough, despite his former protestations about not being a good enough songwriter to fill up an album, all the songs on *Greatest Hits* were written either by Denver or with his collaboration. The big ones were: "Take Me Home, Country Roads," "Follow Me," "Starwood in Aspen," "For Baby (for Bobbie)," "Rhymes & Reasons" (well, not really a genuine greatest hit, admitted Denver, but too beloved by him to be left out), "Leaving, on a Jet Plane," "The Eagle and the Hawk," "Sunshine on My Shoulders," "Goodbye Again," "Poems, Prayers & Promises," and (of course) "Rocky Mountain High." An impressive collection of words and music in anybody's estimation.

Back Home Again, released in August 1974, was John Denver's sweetest—or, depending on your taste, most saccharine—album ever. After "Sunshine on my Shoulders" had been rereleased as a single, it conquered the very top position on all the charts. It was soon followed by another smash hit single, "Annie's Song," the biggest thing on the *Back Home Again* album. "You fill up my senses like a night in a forest," wrote John to his wife, "like the mountains in Springtime, like a walk in the rain, like a storm on the desert, like a sleepy blue ocean, you fill up my senses, come fill me again." Who could resist such an outpouring of romantic love? Almost at once, "Annie's Song" began to replace readings from Kahlil Gibran's *The Prophet* at weddings.

And, not only was "Annie's Song" honored like the theme from *Love Story*, but the Baltimore Orioles baseball team selected "Thank God I'm a Country Boy" to play during their seventh-inning stretch, to the clapping of hands and the stomping of feet.

"Thank God I'm a Country Boy" set the bucolic tone of the entire album. Written by John Martin Sommers, it celebrated country pleasures as clean and fine, and proclaimed that "I'd rather have my fiddle and my farmin' tools . . . than diamonds and jewels." Denver should thank God that nobody ever forced *him* to make that choice. "Hey, it's good to be back home again," sang John. "Sometimes this old farm feels like a long-lost friend," and the glossy strings soar upward.

"Sweet Surrender" was "built on 'Farewell Andromeda,'" stated Denver. "The verses of the song are the problems of living. The chorus is the answer—to flow with life." The song had been written for a Disney film, *The Bears and I*. The movie told the story of a young man who takes his best friend's belongings back to his Indian family after the friend is killed and then adopts three bear cubs. "The Indian feeling is to be one with the earth and live. To me, people think of surrender as someone being forced to give in, to give up and be trapped. True surrender to life is letting life be as it is and you go on doing what you do, being who you are, and what you are. The Indians did this—they believed in passing through, a part of it all, and leaving it the same as it was when they came, taking only what was needed."

Oozing with down-home folksiness and good vibes, *Back Home Again* came off as gushy and sentimental to many critics, but millions rushed out to buy their idol's latest. There was no grit or sand in it, just mellow harmonies, glossy arrangements, and an absolutely flawless sense of commercial viability. It quickly climbed to the platinum

plateau, bearing the John Denver Message to the World: "My purpose in performing is to communicate the joy I experience in living. It is the aliveness already within you that my music is intended to reach. Participating in est has created an amazing amount of space for joy and aliveness in my life. It pleases me to share est with you."

An Evening with John Denver was put together live from the series of concerts he gave at the Universal Amphitheatre in Los Angeles at the end of August, 1974. His first two-record album, it was a convincing demonstration of Denver's talents, and a slickly mounted show. By now he was the top recording artist in the country. RCA Records had posted the best first six-month sales period in its history, and they gave John Denver the lion's share of the credit. The business volume for Denver recordings alone "exceeded the total revenues of many [other] record companies." The album was issued in February of 1975, and shipped both gold and platinum in the first week of issue. By that time, both *John Denver's Greatest Hits* and *Back Home Again* had sold more than three million apiece. (By now, John had five platinum albums and three gold singles within thirteen months.) In one three-day weekend in 1974, more than 400,000 copies of his albums were sold. He was also a ticket-seller of the highest magnitude. Take the Universal Amphitheatre engagement, for example. Within 24 hours of the box office opening, the entire week-long engagement—35,000 seats!—were sold out; many fans had lined up overnight.

An Evening with John Denver combines a lot of the old with some of the new. It wouldn't be a Denver concert without "Take Me Home, Country Roads," "Annie's Song," "Rocky Mountain High," and "The Eagle and the Hawk," but "Jet Plane" and "Sunshine on My Shoulders" were being phased out and do not appear. "My Sweet Lady," which had been recorded on Denver's fourth album, *Poems, Prayers & Promises*, made its reappearance along with other old favorites like "Farewell Andromeda," "Sweet Surrender," and "Thank God I'm a Country Boy." But there were unfamiliar numbers, as well, new songs like "Annie's Other Song" and old ones like Randy Sparks' "Today" and "Saturday Night in Toledo, Ohio"—a satirical look at a sleepy city where you "sit in the park and watch the grass die" or "visit the bakery and watch the buns rise." It never failed to get a rise out of Toledo's Mayor Harry Kessler, who turned a rich shade of purple every time Denver sang it in public.

"My friends," wrote Denver on his *Windsong* album, released in the fall of 1975, "I wanted to record the songs that the wind makes, to play for you between the bands of this album, to share her music with you in the same way that I am able to share mine. In the many hours and days that we spent trying to record all that I hear in the wind, what I found was that you simply can't get it on tape. I hope that, at some time in your life, you'll be able to go someplace where it's quiet, where there are no cars, no dogs barking, no planes passing overhead, and that you will be able to listen to all of the music that she gives us. If you're really lucky, you'll be able to sit by a lake at the foot of a mountain and hear a storm come and go. There is beautiful, beautiful music there. All you have to do is listen. I love you and I wish you peace."

By now he had it all, absolutely all. He was a television personality with his own successful shows, he was *el numero uno* in the shark-infested recording business, he was concertizing with a huge orchestra and split-screen visual effects—he was, in short, a superstar. Only a few months earlier, he had appeared with Frank Sinatra on a twin bill at one of the world's most famous cabarets, Harrah's in Lake Tahoe. He had been named the Poet Laureate of Colorado by the Governor. And he had his son at last; he and Annie had adopted Zachary. He was planning to make at least one Hollywood movie, a musical remake of *Mr. Smith Goes to Washington*, with himself as Smith. He had swept the Country Music Association annual awards, with nominations in five categories (entertainer of the year, male vocalist of the year, song of the year—"Back Home Again," album of the year—*An Evening with John Denver*, and single record of the year—"Thank God I'm a Country Boy"). He'd even won in two of the five categories, entertainer and best song. He had survived his public admission that he smoked hash and grass—although a few parents grew irate and vocal, almost everybody else yawned, so what else is new? He'd been appointed by President Gerald Ford to a presidential advisory committee charged with overseeing the resettlement of an estimated 130,000 Vietnamese refugees in the United States. Two of the singles from his new album, *Windsong*—"I'm Sorry" and "Calypso" (the latter dedicated to Captain Jacques-Yves Cousteau and all who had served on the ship *Calypso*)—were gold records. If there was anybody at any time in the history of the universe who could say "I love you and I wish you peace" to the whole wide record-buying world, that man was John Denver.

JOHN'S TELEVISION CAREER

Colorado Magazine

TWO

Although John Denver's recording and concert career was preparing him for superstardom on the basis of his gold records and song hits, his status was advanced rapidly and enhanced immeasurably by his exposure on television. TV made John Denver into a national institution, a public personality, a household word.

It began simply enough. In the spring of 1972, the British Broadcasting Corporation—BBC— invited Denver to be a guest on Tom Paxton's "In Concert" show. It was a natural choice, and Denver came across as friendly and likable, even chatty. Jerry Weintraub's metal-detector of a brain began to tick gold, and negotiation with the BBC began. Meanwhile, NBC in the United States was planning a rock music show that would go on the air Saturday nights at 1 a.m., when Johnny Carson's "Tonight" signed off. This would be called "The Midnight Special"; the pilot program would have a "Get Out the Vote" theme (it was a Presidential election year) aimed at encouraging the over-eighteen age group to register to vote. Denver, who was coincidentally to be a guest on the Carson show the same night—August 19, 1972— was tabbed to host the "Midnight Special" pilot.

Among John's guests were Cheech and Chong, Argent, Mama Cass Elliott, Linda Ronstadt, Helen Reddy, Mary Travers, and David Clayton-Thomas. The ratings were high, as the show knocked off the opposing networks' Saturday night movies. Acquitting himself well, Denver was on his way to television stardom.

Then the BBC deal came through. Denver was to host a six-week series of *live* variety shows. "Nobody over there knew me and it was a good opportunity to get the experience I needed," Denver recalled. "I found out that I could use the medium to further my music. That's all I'm interested in doing." He was vocally enthusiastic over the challenge that live broadcasting would present. "All live, that's really far out. It adds a whole great pressure. We'll get down to the nitty-gritty and find out if I can do it, what I can do and in what scope. Feeling that I have a career in television in the States, I don't want to blow it."

Impressed by the BBC's handling of good, relatively unknown talent, Denver marveled, "A whole half-hour of John Prine in prime time—there's *nothing* in the States in prime-time TV. Television in the U.S. has become mostly bullshit. And it can destroy you. Look at what happened to Roger Miller—all those hit records, then thirteen weeks on TV and nothing since. And I think the Smothers Brothers were forced into early retirement by TV."

Nonetheless, Denver leaped in and completed six weeks of basic training in front of British audiences. He didn't only sing—he danced, he told stories, he acted as host and comedian. And he was pretty good at just about everything; even his clumsiness as a dancer was almost winning, two left feet having a wholesome charm all their own. The one-hour specials earned high ratings, and Weintraub swung into action in the States.

Returning to the U.S. in the middle of June, 1973, Denver did a substitute-host stint on the "Tonight" show, beating out Dick Cavett and the CBS Late Movie in the same time slot. The he signed a long-term deal with ABC for specials of his own, and went on a concert tour, opening the Universal Amphitheatre season in Los Angeles with a week-long engagement, and playing his first Carnegie Hall gig in New York.

In October of 1972, John's *Rocky Mountain High* album had been released, and it soon went gold, then platinum, giving John two big hits—the title song and "Goodbye Again." His name was now synonymous with mountaintops and eagles, with clean air and a deep love for high country. On the Johnny Carson show, he had established his country-boy "gee-whiz" personality by his lively rapport with his guests, and by the exclamation that was to become his trademark: "Faarrr OUT!" With the studio crew taking bets, and Ed McMahon counting, John uttered those two words some nineteen times in ninety minutes. It had become shtick. "I didn't even realize that I was saying it. When they told me about the bets, I was really embarrassed, but I laughed with everyone else."

Now, the ecological side of Denver was reinforced in the public mind with the broadcasting, in January of 1973, of "Bighorn: Rocky Mountain High," in which Denver, who served as narrator and sang his own songs, teamed up with Tommy Tompkins, ex-detective turned naturalist, to track down the bighorn sheep of the Rockies, a rare and vanishing species. Backpacking through cold as low as minus forty degrees and rafting down rivers, Denver and Tompkins gained rare and exciting footage of the Rockies' wilderness and the natural life there. John sang not only "Rocky Mountain High," but also "Rocky Mountain Suite," "Spring," "Whiskey Basin Blues," and "How Do You Say 'Hello' to a Grizzly Bear?"

"I think a show like this makes people even more aware of wildlife, of the incredible scenery that we as a nation must work to protect. There are so many issues people are concerned about today, but they're all tied in with our environment. And really, ecology starts with the family at home. All of us have to do our part," stated Denver. It was hardly an earth-shattering statement, but nobody could doubt its sincerity.

With "Bighorn: Rocky Mountain High" under his belt, with guest stints on the Merv Griffin Show, the Dick Clark Show, and with Johnny Carson, John's wire-rim glasses, wide grin, and blond Dutch-boy bangs were becoming more and more identifiable by Mr. and Mrs. Middle America. His recognition factor was growing. The broadcasting of a television drama, "Sunshine," gave one more boost to Denver's already booming musical career.

"Sunshine," a two-and-a-half-hour made-for-TV movie, was based on the true story of a very young woman who learned that she was dying of bone cancer, and who kept a diary of her final days. The woman had a deep love for the music of John Denver, and requested that "Take Me Home, Country Roads," which Denver had co-written with Taffy Nivert and Bill Danoff, be played at her funeral. Another of her favorites was "Sunshine on My Shoulders," which lent itself to the film's theme and title. "What amazes me," said John when he performed the song in concert, "is that when the grandparents, the parents, the teenagers, the kids listen to a song like 'Sunshine on My Shoulders,' they all get off. And you gotta know their pictures are all different. But whatever each person out there gets out of a song, that is the absolute truth for that person." The broadcast of "Sunshine" reached a wide audience, as did the eight Denver songs that formed a part of it, and RCA rushed to reissue first a single of "Sunshine," then *Poems, Prayers & Promises*, the album on which "Take Me Home, Country Roads" and "Sunshine on My Shoulders" had first appeared. "Sunshine" reached Number One; the album soon went platinum, and Denver's name was now associated with a celebration of life even in death.

In November of 1973, John did a stint as the guest star on Bob Hope's first television special of the season. Bob donned a Dutch-boy wig and Levis and carried a guitar as a parody of John. By now, Denver's awkwardness had been polished up to *appear* spontaneous; he always knew what would get a laugh, and when "Faarrr OUT!" would be most effective. He was becoming a performer rather than a singer.

Two acting appearances, one on "Owen Marshall," where he made his debut as a lawyer turned rock singer suspected of mercy-killing his mother, and a part in a "McCloud" episode as a deputy sheriff, prepared the masses even more to respond to the very first John Denver ABC-TV special, which was broadcast on March 11, 1974.

Billed months in advance as "The First John Denver Picture Show" and realistically released as "The John Denver Show," the sixty-minute program featured comedy, dancing, and music. John's guests were Lily Tomlin, George Gobel, David Carradine, and James Whitmore, who impersonated Will Rogers. John did his Mr. All-American Nice Guy number, and *Variety* reviewed him as "folksy, naive and genuine." It was, all in all, a pleasant hour; perhaps the most outstanding moment was when John cracked, "Television used to be called the vast wasteland. Now it's only half-vast." Possibly only Mr. Clean John Denver could get away with so bad a double entendre. John sang his big hits, "Rocky Mountain High," and "Sunshine," and came out aggressively on the side of clean air and endangered wildlife, avoiding such controversial topics as mom's apple pie. In addition to singing, John recited a number of syrupy anecdotes about his shyness as an adolescent and his strike-out record with girls, and even danced a few clumsy steps. "I'm trying to expand my horizons," he aw-shucksed, "so I'll be doing a little dancing for the first time and I'll be performing in some of the comedy sketches. The dance thing is a departure for me because it's a Fred Astaire-type number and that tippy-toe stuff isn't too easy to master when you're oriented to being a singer and guitar picker." But it appeared that he could do no wrong.

Almost needless to say, the Colorado Rockies shared the spotlight with John; much of it was filmed on location near the Denver home to lend the country boy a breathtaking backdrop for his mountain music.

John's second special, broadcast in December of 1974, and titled "A Family Event," used Dick Van Dyke, Doris Day, and George Gobel as guests, and presented pretty much the same mixture as before. It really wasn't until his third special, "An Evening with John Denver," that the singer hit his on-camera stride. It was an outstanding program, and it won an Emmy award. Broadcast in March of 1975, the show devoted a large segment of its time to John Denver's visit to Captain Jacques-Yves Cousteau's research vessel, the *Calypso*. With Cousteau, John went underwater exploring the Glover Reef in the Caribbean; the program showed magnificent films of the reef and highlighted the threats facing the survival of reefs all over the world.

Another guest star on "An Evening with John Denver" was Danny Kaye, described by Denver as "a genius." It was Kaye's first appearance on a TV variety show in five years, and thus a real honor for the young entertainer. But the best part of the evening was given over to singing, which was what

Denver was there for. Filmed like a live concert, with John sitting in the middle of the audience and singing his heart out, the musical segment lifted the show above Denver's earlier specials. There was less cuteness, less of a need to show John's so-called "versatility"; the program concentrated on the three most important, most identifiable characteristics: his wholesomeness, his concern for the environment, and his musical talents.

His fourth special, broadcast December 8, 1975, was "Rocky Mountain Christmas," filmed on location in Aspen, Colorado. The same production team that won the Emmy for "An Evening with John Denver"—Al Rogers and Rich Eustis, with Bill Davis as director and the ubiquitous Jerry Weintraub as executive producer—reunited for "Rocky Mountain Christmas." A combination of familiar music and stunning outdoor visuals, it presented awe-inspiring views of the venerable Rockies, and a travelog of Colorado that featured Denver skiing, hiking, singing, and grinning. For those who wanted other pretty scenery to look at, there were Valerie Harper and Olivia Newton-John.

"People want relief from this hectic society of ours," John told reporters before the special was aired, "and that's what we hope to offer them. It provides them with a look at that part of the country that has served as the inspiration for my music." Another part of the program was a pitch to save the grizzly bear, showing some handsome footage of the animal and his part in the balance of nature.

Denver took this opportunity to discuss television in general. "Today they're going for flash instead of quality. People are getting tired of it. They want something that gives meaning to their lives. Of all the current shows, Carol Burnett is the only one I'd watch. As for specials, Perry Como has the classiest show on television." That was hitting Middle America exactly where it lived—in front of its TV set, but the punch was as soft as a marshmallow. About his own type of program, John remarked, "To be in touch with earth is an incredibly valuable thing. It really works for me and through an hour of television we hope to share it with others."

In August of 1975, John had appeared at Harrah's in Lake Tahoe in an unusual one-two combination with none other than Frank Sinatra. Denver had handled the dinner shows (it was assumed, one supposes, that his audiences were known to go to bed early), while Sinatra handled the late crowd (*his* people never went to bed at all; at least, not to sleep). It had been a highly successful engagement and in March 1976 it was to be repeated in prime time; this time, for the TV cameras, the two men—rather, the two superstars—would appear in tandem. It was a blatant confirmation of Denver's growing grip on the polyester-and-hair-spray crowd, Sinatra's territory. Denver had always had the kids and the grandparents in the palm of his guitar-pickin' hand; now he was after the mommies and the daddies, the aunts, the uncles, and the godfathers.

"The thought of this marriage between Hoboken and Aspen, scotch and orange juice," wrote Grace Lichtenstein for the Sunday New York *Times*, "may strike one as intriguing or nauseating. Isn't Denver satisfied with the comfortable niche he's already carved for himself? Isn't he afraid of rupturing his identity or hurting his clean-cut image? 'I don't care,' he responds disarmingly. 'I intend to expand and to grow, period. I'm not afraid of losing any audience, as long as there are people who find value in what I'm doing.'"

It was the same old theme that Denver had been quoting for years, but as one watched the special—which had him dancing in rhinestone-studded costumes with chorus boys and girls, which dragged out the exhausted television-variety cliché of having two very different singers try out each other's songs—one could not help thinking. If there was one quote that had been circulated more widely than any other, one pearl which fell more continually from Denver's sincere lips than any other, it was this: "I don't want to merely entertain people, I want to touch them. That's where it's at with me."

IN CONCERT

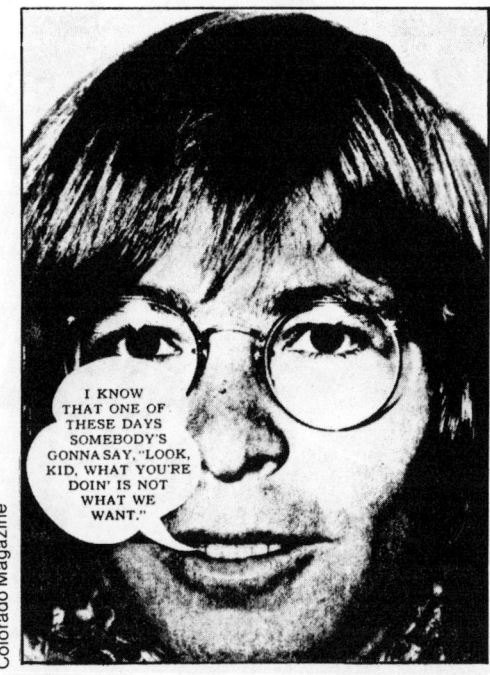

Colorado Magazine

THREE

"Playing before an audience is what I do best," said John Denver more than once. "Recording gives you a chance to get it down exactly the way you want it and preserve it that way. But an audience gives so much back to you. I think my concerts do well at colleges because so many other musicians have put the kids on, and I don't. I like to think I do a *show*, and I select songs for a purpose, songs I think mean something. I can't see running yourself ragged trying to be on top of the latest trend. I expect to be able to make my living this way a long time—all my life."

But John's concerts have changed a great deal. He no longer plays intimate halls; he can't afford to, with ticket demand so very great. His shows have become longer and larger and more intricately mounted, with a warm-up act (for years he played without one), a twenty-six piece orchestra, and strong visuals on a giant three-fold screen. "The problem lies," he told Jared Johnson of the Houston *Post*, "in your getting to the point where you're working toward getting larger audiences, to get through to as many people as possible. But if you do the type of show that I do, you like it to be close and intimate, so you're sort of working against yourself. So what you try to do . . . the problem involved is to make a large house like this feel like they're sitting in your living room, and that's what I'm working for. That's the way I like it to be. Loose and close.

"I tell my audiences before each show that I would like them to relax, enjoy themselves and go wherever the music takes them. Now that's a tiny little statement, but it opens up a space for a lot of people to let the pictures that music creates *come*."

John's early concerts were models of simplicity and sincerity. He recited/sang "America the Beautiful," for example, and it was obvious to all that he meant every word of it. In 1972, he was still incorporating Tom Paxton's antiwar ballad, "Jimmy Newman," into every concert. He concertized at Carnegie Hall, together with Fat City (Denver's friends Bill Danoff and Taffy Nivert) and Megan McDonough. He presented his Middle America image to the notoriously blasé New York audiences and they ate it up, giving him a standing ovation and calling for more.

On his spring 1973 tour, John was still facing his audiences virtually by his lonesome, backed only by Dick Kniss on bass and Paul Prestopino on six- and twelve-string guitar. His repertory leaned heavily on the work of other composers, such as Prine, Paxton, and Brel (his version of Jacques Brel's "Amsterdam" usually brought down the house), but he also did his own most successful songs—"Country Roads," "Leaving, on a Jet Plane," "Rocky Mountain High"—as he worked toward completing his own identity. Holding the stage for more than two and a half hours, John delivered again and again; socking his audiences with his wholesome personality as well as his music, and making certain to give his fans the Denver "mix" of old, familiar numbers that he was identified with, and new material that he wanted to bring to a wider audience.

One of the musical highlights of 1973 was Geraldo Rivera's "One to One" concert at Madison Square Garden on May 31. Proclaimed "One to One Day" by New York's Mayor John Lindsay, May 31 was dedicated to helping the mentally retarded children of New York's Willowbrook State Hospital. An incredible array of musical talent donated their services to make the concert outstanding; the audience packed Madison Square Garden, and the concert raised more than $180,000. John Denver flew in from London (where he was in the midst of his live TV specials for the BBC) especially to appear on the same stage with Judy Collins, Sly Stone, Kris Kristofferson and Rita Coolidge, Richie Havens, Eric Weissberg and Deliverance, Bill Withers, and Peter, Paul and Mary. But it was John's forty-five-minute set, during which he sang "Take Me Home, Country Roads," "Rocky Mountain High," and "I'd Rather Be a Cowboy," that was the highlight of the evening, topped only by the ten-minute rendition of Dylan's "Blowin' in the Wind," sung by the legendary folk trio of Peter, Paul and Mary, reunited especially for this charitable occasion and joined by all the other artists. "One to One" was a stunning occasion, and it brought Denver much glory and good publicity, as well as a sense of satisfaction.

"Lots of people write me off as little Mr. Innocent, but they get quite a surprise when they come to my concerts expecting to see the All-American boy, and gritty me shows up," said John in 1973. He repeated this statement as late as spring 1976, on the Merv Griffin television show, even though it had long been only a shadow of the truth. "Gritty me," with his Tom Paxton antiwar songs, had virtually disappeared by his celebrated Universal Amphitheatre appearance in July 1973.

During that week-long stint in Hollywood, which played to sold-out, enthusiastic houses, "gritty me" was backed up not only by his own five-man group (acoustic and steel guitars, banjo, harmonica, stand-up bass, drums and piano) but also by the Amphitheatre's thirty-piece orchestra, which was heavy on the strings, and which sometimes overpowered Denver's simplicity with an overdose of sweetness. "Visually, as well as lyrically," wrote the *Hollywood Reporter*, "the singer is packaged nature." All the reviews of this week-long engagement made mention of the vast three-part screen onto which were projected films of the majestic Rockies, of the eagle and the hawk, the canyons and the trees, and Denver himself. The slide show was integrated into the concert, making the entire presentation an audio-visual trip to Colorado.

Bruce Ditchfield

By 1974, John Denver had become the compleat entertainer—a recording superstar, a television personality recognizable all over America. His concert audiences were so clean and well-behaved that, in recognition, the state of Nevada declared that it no longer considered Denver a rock star. In Nevada, rock musicians are compelled to post a $5,000 bond before they can play large halls, such is the destructive enthusiasm of their audiences. But Denver, announced Bill Harrison of the Centennial Coliseum in Reno, was a "gentleman," who drew a "well-balanced and attentive" audience, therefore he should be designated an "entertainer" rather than a rock star, and should not have to post bond.

John Denver's shows had by then taken on the trappings of a full-scale production—the triple screen, a twenty-six-piece orchestra that included twenty-two strings, his five sidemen, Bill Danoff and Taffy Nivert, and even a spot of juggling. John kept three oranges more or less going in the air, just to show his versatility and give the crowd a laugh. Every show included a pitch for the preservation of wilderness and wildlife, loving references to his wife, his home in the Rockies and his pets. The show ran long, over two and a half hours, and John was onstage virtually all of that time, singing his heart out with obvious relish. He had established a tremendous rapport with his audiences, and his shows were truly a

visit with the man himself.

Critics of the Denver show considered his presentations too slick, too schmaltzy, too crowd-pleasing, and overorchestrated—a symphony of homespun hokum and calculated simplicity. But there was no doubt that John's audiences were uncritical; they devoured his folksy banter, his cries of "Faarrr OUT!" and even his juggling. The most striking portion of his two and a half hour long concerts was generally conceded to be "The Eagle and the Hawk," sung stirringly by Denver against a background of magnificent color film of the swooping, soaring birds. The film seemed to be the living embodiment of the freedom sought in Denver's lyrics.

Also, John had taken to ending his concerts on a very special note. Standing alone on stage, playing a simple acoustic guitar as his only accompaniment, John would sing "This Old Guitar" as his final number, leaving his audience with a picture not of the grandeur of the mountains but of the simplicity of the man instead. It provided just the right dramatic ending for the evening's entertainment. He had come a long way from the old Troubadour or Greek Theatre days. Although he still sang "Spanish Pipedream" and "When I'm Sixty-Four," the heart and soul of his work now was his own songs, rather than the compositions of others. And, in his striking visuals, he provided an escape from city cares and pollution, taking his audience into an idyllic environment of peaceful, lyrical cleanliness.

Another impressive fact about Denver was that he continued to concertize heavily, even when his albums and his TV appearances had made him so rich and famous that many another artist in the same situation would give up the grueling concert schedule and make only rare appearances. John still got off on live audiences, reaching out to everybody within the sound of his voice. In the fall of 1974 he launched a twenty-one-city tour from Portland, Oregon, a tour that included his debut in the massive Madison Square Garden.

And, in the spring of 1975, John headed off on the biggest national tour of one-nighters in his career—thirty concerts in twenty-nine cities. John dubbed the tour "Celebrate," but those connected with it knew it more as the "six-million-dollar tour," and with good reason. Why was the tour called "Celebrate"? "Because it will be spring," said Denver, "and everything will be beautiful. And we hope to make it an uplifting experience for everyone."

For the first time in six years of touring, John used an opening act, Liberty. Having recently formed his own record label, Windsong, John was recording the country-rock group Liberty, the first group he'd signed, friends of his from Aspen. In addition to his usual backup band, the tour featured a full orchestra, known as Galaxy. His second tour within eight months, it showed Denver at his indefatigable best, zestful, friendly, energetic and optimistic—he'd sing in the neighborhood of twenty-five songs per concert, holding the stage for the greatest part of the long program, and obviously relishing both the spotlight and the audience rapport. He was in his "bluegrass period," so "Grandma's Feather Bed" and "Thank God I'm a Country Boy" formed an important part of the repertoire, as did some fancy country pickin' together with Steve Weisberg and John Sommers of the backup band.

In August of 1975, Denver brought a slightly scaled-down version of his concert program to Lake Tahoe, where he appeared for a week with Frank Sinatra (Denver did the early shows and Frank the late ones) at Harrah's. Playing to packed houses in his first nightclub engagement, John chortled, "Boy, this is pretty far out! It's a far cry from the old Cellar Door in Washington, D.C., and the Golliwog Lounge in Minneapolis."

Standing room only, back to back with the most famous singer in America, Frank Sinatra—John Denver had indeed come a long, long way in a short time. "Sinatra is the King," crowed Jerry Weinberg, who had put the Lake Tahoe deal together. "Who's the Crown Prince? John Denver is the Crown Prince. The great contrast is Denver and Sinatra. Yet, when you think about it, Denver is a crooner of the

seventies. Now that's not a putdown. Denver appeals to a very very wide audience, the way Crosby did in the forties, the way Sinatra did in the fifties, the way Presley did in the sixties. And John Denver does it in the seventies.

"All seven nights were sold out five minutes after the announcement was made. Last night, when Frank said about John's show, 'A new nightclub star is born and God knows we need one,' that's very important."

From the tiny club to the concert stage to the amphitheatre and back to the club, only this time on the grandest nightclub scale possible—in one decade Denver had gone from a modest folkie to the superstar of his generation.

AT HOME IN COLORADO

Colorado Magazine

FOUR

He was born in the summer of his 27th year,
comin' home to a place he'd never been before....

I never had a home, a place that was mine, something I wanted more than anything else in the world. We've built one in Aspen, Colorado. I love the mountains. I feel uncomfortable in cities most of the time, and the first time I went there, Aspen felt a lot more like home than any other place I'd ever been."

On seven acres of rocky green land, high above Aspen, in an exclusive residential community called Starwood where celebrities like Jill St. John and Spider Sabich and Claudine Longet made their home, John and Annie Denver built their dream house. Of wood and glass, with a glass-enclosed loft where John can watch the shooting stars and the flights of eagles, the $150,000 three-bedroom split-level dwelling was raised. "It's quite contemporary, all wood and glass," said John happily. "It's very open, so that you can be involved with people."

But what people? Starwood has its own private guard complete with guardhouse, and John posted a sign on his property that read: "PLEASE Do Not Bother Us. You Are Not Welcome Here. *Thank You*." There was a spate of bad publicity when the sign became public knowledge, and the Denvers took it down. Yet, are they not entitled to

their privacy?

"Home is not my work," explained Denver. "So many people come by who want to talk to me, take a picture, whatever. And each one thinking he's the only one who's taken the time to find the house. If he only knew.

"I have a handmower, and I like to go out on a sunny day, when nobody is around, take all my clothes off, and mow my yard. When I was growing up, there weren't many yards, and I wasn't into working them anyway. But this—this is *mine!* My yard, right there in the mountains, and I stand there naked, and look around and think, I'm not on vacation! I live here! It blows my mind. That's home. That and Annie. Everything we do is play. That's how it should be.

"When I'm at home in Aspen some days I get up at dawn, especially now with Zach. I like getting up when he gets up and feeding him and playing with him in the morning before everybody else gets up. And sometimes I just sleep in. When I'm home I really need time to myself. I need time to play and this is something that I recognized in my own life. A lot of people get stuck into thinking that you're a grownup now and you can't play, you can't waste time. There's no such thing as wasting time in my dictionary. I like to play and I like to be out in the mountains. I like to ride my motorcycle, and I'm really gettin' off on learning how to fly. I love to listen to music and I don't like to go home and sit down and start dealing with business."

Now his life is full of wonder, but his heart still knows some fear / Of a simple thing he cannot comprehend. Why they try to tear the mountain down to bring in a couple more / More people, more scars upon the land.

Trouble in Paradise. Ever since John Denver began publicly praising and immortalizing Colorado's pure air, clean water and majestic scenery, tourists—especially young ones—have been overrunning the once empty landscape. Long's Peak in Estes Park is filled to bursting with backpackers and Aspen has become a tourist resort. When every five minutes on the radio tells you about the joys of the Rockies and of "sitting round the campfire and everybody's high," who can blame you for wanting to go and find out for yourself? There are a growing number of Colorado residents who grind their teeth in impotent rage whenever Big-Mouth Denver's name is mentioned.

"The whole damn state has gone public since he's been advertising it," growled one angry citizen. The *Colorado Daily*, a Boulder paper, recently held a "When I First Realized I Hated John Denver" contest. "He's a carpetbagger," said a Colorado advertising man. "He's only lived here a few years and he has no idea, no comprehension, of what this state is really about. People are moving in and pretty soon our welfare rolls are going to start growing, like in Hawaii, which was promoted as a paradise and now has the highest percentage on welfare in the country."

"That twerp sits up in his $150,000 mountain home and writes songs about how beautiful it is to live in Colorado," said an embittered Denver folksinger. "I'd like to see him come down where I live on East Colfax and write about how groovy it is."

Yet everybody agrees that John Denver is a once-in-a-lifetime phenomenon; they couldn't have invented him as a P.R. man for Colorado if they'd tried. He's not, after all, trying to sell real estate. He sings about his own life and his own dreams of happiness, and they are inevitably entwined with Colorado.

With their roots sunk deep in Colorado rock, John and Annie were able to realize their most poignant wish. For years unable to have children of their own, they recently adopted a baby boy, Zachary. They had been married for eight years when, in May 1974, John Denver had a dream. "I've always had this idea that the relationship between parents and a baby is that all three are looking for each other, seeking each other out, before the baby is born. I dreamed about this one particular baby. When he smiled, you could see the gums in his wide, sensual mouth. I came back home and the adoption agency called and said they had a baby for us."

JOHN DENVER Exclusively on RCA

RCA Records and Tapes

When he and Annie went to pick up the baby, Denver told interviewer Dick Kleiner, the adoption agency officials marveled. "They said they had never seen anything like it. They were amazed at how the baby seemed to smile at us as though he were greeting old friends. And the mouth of the baby was just like the mouth in the baby of my dream—wide and sensual and you could see the gums."

Oh, we want to call him Zachary, and we'll raise him in the mountains / And he'll bathe in crystal fountains, shining laughter in the sun.

"Zachary is the best thing that ever happened to me. I think kids enhance everything. I no longer see anything or experience anything that doesn't bring with it a picture of either sharing the experience with Zachary, when I can communicate it to him, or thinking about him growing into that same experience.

"Moving to the mountains and discovering myself is like being born again. Born again, a totally religious thing that had nothing to do with the church." Now that Zach has made them a real family—husband and wife, child, two dogs and three cats—John feels his life is perfect. "I'm really aware of the perfection of my life. There's a lot more I'm responsible for, or maybe I'm aware more of the responsibility that I have, but I'm doing what I've always wanted to do." He has said that if the show business thing ever gets stale or peters out, he and Annie will open a restaurant in Colorado. Annie will cook, and John will sing and wait on tables. "And I'll find no less joy there than in what I'm doing now. I love this work. I love meeting people and I love being on stage. I have so much fun up there. But as soon as it stops, or reaches a level, I'll go back to the mountains."

A restaurant! What a fantasy!

DENVER AND EST

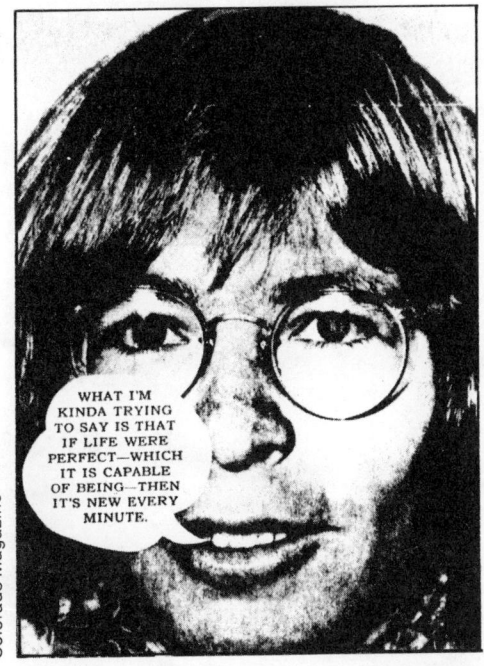

FIVE

When John Denver speaks, as he often does, of "creating a space" for his life and his music, of "moving through" his problems, or of "aliveness," he is using the language of Werner Erhard and est, or Erhard Seminar Training, a discipline to which he subscribes wholeheartedly, a discipline that stresses self-awareness and the responsibility for one's own life.

"Werner developed est by incorporating the things that work in other disciplines such as yoga and Zen. Est means "it is" in Latin. It's helped me understand who I am, why I am and why I'm where I am." On the *Windsong* album, John dedicated "Looking for Space" "to Werner Erhard and everyone in est." "On the road of experience," it goes, "I'm trying to find my own way . . . . And I'm looking for space, and to find out who I am, And I'm looking to know and understand. . . . Sometimes I fly like an eagle and sometimes I'm deep in despair."

John talked about est at length with Chet Flippo of *Rolling Stone*. "I can't tell you what est is and I say that in a way that I can't tell you what that experience was. I can only tell you what my experiences are since then; I can tell you what my experiences are out of est and they are totally supportive of me being—who I am. I think it's really far out to realize that it's

okay to be who you are.

"Est is Erhard Seminar Training and that's what it's called because you can't call an organization in California est [est originated in San Francisco] but you can call something Erhard Seminar Training and the guy who came up with est or put it together is Werner Erhard. He's a few years older than I am and comes from a little bit different background and was operating in a little bit different area—which was mostly motivation and stuff and he has a very disciplined mind. He got into a lot of disciplines, and, it seems to me, took what worked out of this one, what worked out of that one and all the stuff that didn't work he threw away and then put it all together and came up with something that works very, very efficiently.

"See, the first time Werner came to Aspen, before he did the first training there, I walked out; I though it was total bullshit, a rip-off. Pushed all my buttons, man, and I walked out. Later they had a training in Aspen and some people I'd seen there, there was something different, and I don't know that it was good or bad, wrong or right or any of those things, but something happened and I was really in this space of looking, really looking. In fact, a lot of people who have taken the training thought that I wrote the *Rocky Mountain High* album after the training and the truth is that I had finished the album before I took the training. But the thing is, I saw that something had happened and so then they were gonna have another training and I was gonna be there at that time and I was very interested and so I took the training and I really think that I took the training in a perfect space because I wasn't expecting anything from it and I wasn't there to put it down or to make it wrong to prove it wasn't gonna work for me. I just wanted to find out what happened. And est really clarified a lot of notions.

"I think it enhanced my awareness—through some tools that I found in the est training, tools that were presented that allowed me to really take a look at things that I can use everyday. For instance, I find that people get stuck—like we were talking yesterday and talked about music and today about finding out what works. You got something that's working for you, man, *go* with that. You got something that's not working and there are a million signs you get that it's not working. Then either alter it to make it work or get out of it. Change it or leave it."

There is so pervading a vagueness, so thick a fog of elusive verbiage in this interview that one wonders whether Chet's recorder batteries were running down, or whether his tape heads were covered with fur. But that's est. That's they way those who have been through the training avoid describing it; it's like giving away secret lodge handshakes and passwords. Denver's evasiveness as to what really happens in the seminars is universal, which accounts for those books about it becoming bestsellers. It's the only way our curiosity can be appeased.

"Est is just about the most interesting thing I've come across. It's really mind-blowing, far out, and it *works.* Simply, it works. I have a sense that I'm doing the same kind of thing, in my concerts, and that's the space that's available to me now, and I have no desire to walk away from it; Werner's a beautiful man, and I love him, and I support him totally in what he's doing. I support est totally."

DENVER TALKS ABOUT HIS MUSIC & OTHERS'

IF I'VE EVER SEEN A PHONY ON TELEVISION, IT'S JOHNNY CASH... A GUY I ADMIRE AND RESPECT AS AN ENTERTAINER.

SIX

"I want my music to take people away from the harshness of reality. Away from songs like 'Sister Morphine' [the Rolling Stones]. I want people to feel the goodness in their own lives. It's funny, but I have this capacity to make people happy. I can make them smile. I really am an oddity."

"Do you see much happiness up on stage when you see the Rolling Stones? There's always people who're gonna get off on pain and weirdness, but just as much as they get off on that—and there seems to be a great deal of that going around these days—there's also a great desire people have to be happy.... Lots of freaks might invite James Taylor into their living rooms, but I don't think Middle America would."

"I know I'm no Bob Dylan as a songwriter, there's no way I'm a Bob Dylan. And I'm not James Taylor or Kris Kristofferson. And I would give anything in—no, I would *not* give anything in the world, but I'd love to write some songs like I think they write. But I don't do that. I'd love to be able to sing like Harry Nilsson, David Clayton-Thomas, some of those people, but I don't sing like that. I don't have a very lyrical voice, if that's the word. But I'm a great entertainer."

"What I sing about is what I know. That's where the music comes from. I'm not trying to make life anything it isn't. What I'm tring to do is communicate what is so about my life. What I feel. Every once in a while, you realize what is so for you.

You need to look inside yourself. When you find out what your truth is, you are on top of life. The truth is not what you see. The truth is what you think about what you see."

"I used to wonder how I would feel about working, going on tour, after achieving everything that was really important to me. And I've found that more than anything else I want to share this joy in my life because I see an absence of it everywhere else."

"A lot of people object to the optimism in my music. But if you listen to my records, you hear about things that trouble me. To me life is a bed of roses but I'm also aware that there are things that make me angry and afraid. Not for myself, but for our way of life, our country. Not every song I've written is 'Rocky Mountain High.' The reason I stay optimistic is that everything is new every time I do it. I've never cut this record before. I've sung the same songs a thousand times, but I've never done the concert I'm going to do. It's brand-new, man, let's go out and see what this one is like!"

"I don't write the songs. I just get out of the way and let the music flow through me. I never, for instance, wanted to be a rock star. All I wanted was to represent the music that goes through me, that I feel, and I don't want to do anything that gets in the way of it. The feedback I get from other people acknowledges the fact that they get something out of it."

"My perfect song is 'Rocky Mountain High.' I couldn't change one word or note of it to make it better. It says exactly what I want it to say. Many people think it's a dope song. When I write a dope song, everyone will know it's a dope song."

"I'm not an Alice Cooper, David Bowie or Mick Jagger. They're theatre people—I'm an entertainer. I find that a lot of people who come out of a Mick Jagger concert feel frustrated and empty. After my concerts, people come up to me and say 'wow! what a far out evening!' Those people have felt something and they'll go on feeling something."

"The problem with many of the electric groups is that eighty percent of their albums is pure crap. There is no communication with the audience. Groups like the New York Dolls and David Bowie exist only to please the far-out and sick. Alice Cooper entertains a lot of people, but in two or three years he won't be around."

"I would love to be a songwriter like Bob Dylan or James Taylor or Kris Kristofferson or Carole King. I said this to my brother last night. I would love to write something that is going to be remembered and mean something. But I'm not Bob Dylan! I'm no John Prine—Jesus! I think

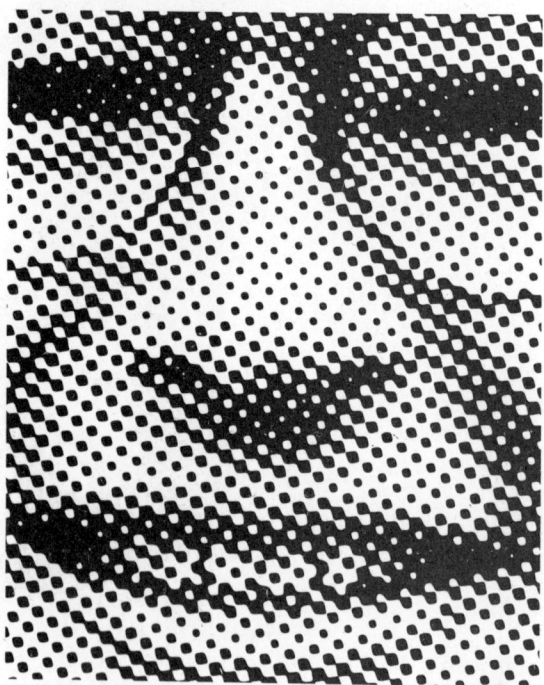

he's a great writer. I think I've written some good songs. I think 'Leaving, on a Jet Plane' is a good song. I think 'Follow Me' is a good song. I think 'Rocky Mountain High' might be a really good song.

"But one who is labeled a songwriter is one whose primary effort is involved in writing songs. Kris Kristofferson, as far as I'm concerned, has no business on stage performing his own songs. He's boring. He's a horrible singer and he has to get drunk to do it. Bob Dylan is a little bit more of a performer and an entertainer. Still, he is a songwriter. From that, all the other stuff came.

"Neil Diamond calls himself a songwriter. Evidently, he *is* a songwriter.

His songs have moved a great deal of people. He's very, very successful. He's probably the most successful singer-songwriter in the business today. I can't remember two lines from any song he's written with the possible exception of 'Songs sung blue, everybody knows one / Every garden grows one.' And I can't tell you the rest of that song."

"Glen Campbell had a couple of years but people got tired of him, because if I've ever seen a phony, he's it. Although I do think he's a great guitar player and a pretty good singer. And if I've ever seen a phony on television, it's Johnny Cash, who happens to be a guy I admire and respect as a great entertainer—but man, not on television."

"I think people see themselves in me. The music is of a kind that touches people of all different ages, from all different backgrounds. People are finding value in it that's more than just entertainment, more than just pretty. For a long time now it hasn't been okay to acknowledge certain things about yourself. For example, that you love your old lady. That it feels good to be out in the sunshine. That every once in a while on a rainy day you feel sad. That life is good. As I have been able to communicate those things for myself and to reach a large audience, that gives them support in feeling those things. Nobody else is singing these songs. Everybody else is talking about how hard life is, and here I am singing about how good it is to be alive!"

DENVER VS. THE CRITICS

Photograph by Francesco Scavullo

SEVEN

"A Denver concert in a big city," wrote Barry Gewen in *Viva*, "is almost certain to draw two things: a sellout crowd and a bad review." And, certainly, John Denver has had his share—perhaps more—of barbed words from the writing fraternity. But his country-boy persona, his scrubbed and shining innocent optimism and, above all, all those millions upon millions of dollars he earns makes him so visible a target. It's almost irresistible, because you know the poor guy is going to cry all the way to Fort Knox. It almost seems that nobody loves John Denver but the people."

"Denver manages to make even the best material feel just a bit unfulfilling," wrote Don Heckman in the New York *Times* in 1972. "His own songs are mostly dreamy evocations about the joys of mountain streams and cool, clean air—pleasant enough thoughts but ultimately so saccharine as to be soporific."

Bob Claypool of the Houston *Post* attended a sold-out concert in early 1973, and noted that the crowd seemed to love it. But as for himself, "If the Friday night concert proved anything to me, it was that ninety percent of [Denver's] material is nothing more than schmaltzy, repetitious corn couched in 'love-your-brother' platitudes. In the end, his music is more contemporary Muzak than contemporary folk.... Strangely enough, all of the numbers he sang (even the gutsy ones composed by other people) came out sounding the same; all were subdued, whitewashed and filtered through his saccharine delivery. . . . To make matters even worse, Denver's second-rate brotherly-love sentiments, delivered through his lyrics, helped fill the auditorium with a smug air of sophisticated sanctimony. It was that old Philosophy of Hip all over again—there's Us in here, all cuddly and warm and Right, and then there are those planet-polluting yokels (Them) out there."

"The latest installment of the Denver Method for turning the brain to apple butter includes some of the most offensively maudlin and contrived images since little Lucy Grey got whisked off to heaven by the presumable angels," growled Freddy Bosco of Denver Colorado in his review of the album *Back Home Again,* the production of which he criticized as "thick, lush and replete with a Supermarket Orchestra and choruses of heavy breathing."

Loraine Alterman of the New York *Times* was another sniper at that album, marking out the title cut and "Annie's Song" as being especially "lightweight" and "banal." "What bothers me most about Denver's music is that it's so boring," she wrote, complaining that Denver settled "for a corny sentimentality that just doesn't register on any deep level."

Nor was the Los Angeles *Times* far behind its eastern colleague in the carping department. "Denver's tendency toward sugar-coated glimpses of life," wrote Robert Hilburn, "has often left critics a bit cold—his lyrics lack the insight and urgency of our finest contemporary writers (Dylan, Mitchell, Prine, Browne)—his music all too often reflects only one side. It is nice to sing about the Rocky Mountains and sunshine, but what about the trouble of the cities and the despair that surrounds so much of modern life? It is costing him credibility with much of the contemporary pop music market."

Joel Selvin remarked in the San Francisco *Chronicle* in February of 1974 that Denver's "insipid songs are to serious contemporary folk music what Kahlil Gibran's writings are to serious literature. His precious low-brow songs all deal with similarly pastoral themes: wildlife conservation, the great outdoors, the search for peace and truth. He's a regular guitar-toting Henry Thoreau."

"You've got to admit the boy's cheerful," said Lynn Van Matre in the Chicago *Tribune.* "A more cheerful singer-songwriter, in fact, would be hard to find. For starters, imagine Glen Campbell with a coat hanger in his mouth. Throw in a megadose of sunshine (the natural variety), some sugar-cured ham, great lungfuls of that euphoria-producing mountain air, and enough chitchat to program a thousand Chatty Kathy dolls, and you've got it."

And when Larry Rohter, a pop music critic for the Washington *Post*, reviewed Denver unflatteringly for that paper, letters in defense of their idol came pouring in from indignant fans. Rohter had asked rhetorically why John Denver was America's favorite singer, pointing out that "cornflakes and potato chips, which contain as much substance and nourishment as Denver's product, are popular too. John Denver, a fair guitarist, an earnest but mediocre singer, an insufferably cloying lyricist, doesn't have much to offer musically, so there must be something else to explain his extraordinary appeal." Rohter went on to blame the singer's appeal on his uncritical audience, which was "more familiar with Disney World than who's on the cover of *Rolling Stone*." Stung, the uncritics scrambled to reply; one reader suggested that everybody at the *Post*, Rohter leading the way, be taken out and shot, while another defended Disney World from the slanders of its attacker. But in the main, the letters said that John Denver and his music brought them pleasure and made them happy, the very claim—and *only* claim—that Denver himself makes for himself.

In his *Viva* article, Barry Gewen analyzed Denver's music and came up with a unique theory, that Denver is "the paradigm of a current musical trend that for want of a better name might be called Prot (i.e., Protestant) Rock." In rock 'n' roll, the Rolling Stones' Mick Jagger is Satan, an evil force exemplifying the raunch of the music. "But the Prot

Rockers—among them Denver, [Don] McLean, Jim Croce, Seals and Crofts, Loggins and Messina, the Eagles—attempted to save the music they loved by cleaning it up, putting Old Satan behind them. Prot Rock is missionary music, the sound that purifies. Unfortunately, what was seen as evil by McLean and the others—dynamism, sexuality, Dionysian vitality—was to a large degree the essence of rock music, and what the Prot Rockers have succeeded in creating is an undiluted sweetness entirely lacking in substance.

"Prot Rock destroys the very thing it tries to save, and consequently has little room for future development. Neither rock nor soul nor country can, in fact, move in only one direction: Listen closely to 'Sunshine on My Shoulders' and you will hear the strains of the 1957 hit 'Tammy.' John Denver may be Pollyanna today; tomorrow he will be Debbie Reynolds."

Robert Christgau, the eminent rock music critic, had begun by liking Denver's delivery, but later he attacked him as a "rank hypocrite." "He's written a few good songs and he is a very professional entertainer," he wrote in the *Village Voice*. "But his philosophical concept of the world—selling the notion of pastoral isolation to a mass audience—is so full of contradictions I can't believe he doesn't see it himself."

But the most excoriating and perhaps the most eloquent attack on John Denver and his music, his philosophy, and his way of life was printed in *Creem*, the rock and roll magazine. In its pages he was creemed by Lester Bangs. "There is nothing so destructive to any piety as making it the object of kitsch, and John Denver is kitsch at apogee . . . there is nothing so degrading as wallowing in apple pie. . . . John Denver is one of those who . . . destroy the System by boring from within. He does this by being boring, and by reducing everything connected with possessing a sense of wonder about things in the natural world to the level of a bad joke. He deals in a certain worship of the elements, he *markets* that worship, and . . . he turns the awesome beauty of a sunset into banal trash. . . . Unfortunately for everybody who ever watched an American eagle soar above a Rocky Mountain, John will soon have us all so sick of eagles *and* clear snow-peaks that it won't even matter that the old bird is expiring in a moulting mulch. . . ."

What Lester Bangs was suggesting was that John Denver is the prime candidate for Godhead: "a huckster who doesn't know, the Manchurian Candidate, stupid enough to hype Werner Erhard, a magical innocent who cheapens, and thereby destroys, everything he thinks he is celebrating and preserving, every time he opens his mouth. Under such conditions, it is nothing that he owns seven separate mountains in Colorado—this man owns the American Dream, and is thankfully doing it to death by selling it at top dollar, which is what it was designed for in the first place."

In the face of such determined onslaughts over the years—termed saccharine, bland, mediocre, boring, banal, monotonous, corny—what has John Denver had to say in his own defense? "The guy who wrote the review," he said once, referring to an unfavorable writeup of a concert in Denver, "said he couldn't find any relevance in my music. You know why? Because his life is probably a drag. He can't tell if it's sunny outside or raining because of the smog. If he wants his life to be a drag, it's all right with me. Critics don't mean a thing to me. When I'm raising a family and enjoying life in the mountains on a full-time basis, they won't matter then, either."

But critics *do* mean a thing to all performers and Denver is no exception. He admitted as much in *Rolling Stone* when he said, "I sometimes get upset by reviews. I think it's one of my weaknesses, one of the things I haven't quite gotten through yet. . . . People who would review a concert and out of 18,000 people one guy would write a review, and I know that 17,999 people were at a different concert than that guy was at—but, see, that's the concert that *he* was at. I resent it or used to resent it and maybe I still do. This is one of the things I need to get through, that people, quite often critics and reviewers, editorialize as opposed to review. . . . If they just said, now this is how I felt as opposed to this is the way it was, because I feel that I've gotten some of the worst reviews of concerts and albums that I've read."

Yet, bad reviews or good, there is never an empty seat and nobody's albums sell better than Denver's, not even Elton John's. It seems that Denver—like many of us—is a man with a great need to be loved by everybody, even critics and reviewers.

DISCO-
GRAPHY

Take Me to Tomorrow - *(RCA #LSP-4278)*. 1970

"Take Me to Tomorrow"
"Isabel"
"Follow Me"
"Forest Lawn"
"Aspenglow"
"Amsterdam"
"Anthem—Revelation"
"Carolina in My Mind"
"Sticky Summer Weather"
"Jimmy Newman"
"Molly'

Whose Garden Was This - *(RCA #LSP-4414)*. 1970

"Tremble If You Must"
"Sail Away Home"
"The Night They Drove Old Dixie Down"
"Mr. Bojangles"
"I Wish I Could Have Been There (Woodstock)"
"Whose Garden Was This"
"The Game Is Over"
"Eleanor Rigby"
"Old Folks"
Medley: "Golden Slumbers," "Sweet Sweet Life," "Tremble if You Must (Version II)," "Jingle Bells"

Beginnings - *(Mercury #SRM 1-704)*. 1974
(Originally released as **That's The Way It's Gonna Be** - *SR-61049*, August 1965; and **Violets of Dawn** - *SR-61067*, December 1965).

by The Mitchell Trio

"That's The Way It's Gonna Be"
"For Bobbi"
"Another Side of This Life"
"Bells of Rhymney"
"Never Coming Home"
"Get Together"
"Mr Tambourine Man"
"Like To Deal With the Ladies"
"Rabbit"
"She Loves You"
"Long Tall Texan"
"Violets of Dawn"

Rhymes & Reasons - *(RCA #LSP-4207)*. 1969

"The Love of the Common People"
"Catch Another Butterfly"
"Daydream"
"The Ballad of Spiro Agnew"
"Circus"
"When I'm Sixty-Four"
"The Ballad of Richard Nixon"
"Rhymes & Reasons"
"Yellow Cat"
"Leaving, on a Jet Plane"
"(You Dun Stomped) My Heart"
"My Old Man"
"I Wish I Knew How It Would Feel To Be Free"
"Today Is the First Day of the Rest of My Life (Sugacity)"

Poems, Prayers & Promises - *(RCA #LSP-4499)*. 1971

"Poems, Prayers & Promises"
"Let It Be"
"My Sweet Lady"
"Wooden Indian"
"Junk"
"Gospel Changes"
"Take Me Home, Country Roads"
"I Guess He'd Rather Be in Colorado"
"Sunshine on My Shoulders"
"Around and Around"
"Fire and Rain"
"The Box"

Aerie - *(RCA #LSP-4607).* 1972 (Spring)

"Starwood in Aspen"
"Everyday"
"Casey's Last Ride"
"City of New Orleans"
"Friends with You"
"60 Second Song for a Bank, with the Phrase 'May We Help You Today?' "
"Blow Up Your TV (Spanish Pipe Dream)"
"All of My Memories"
"She Won't Let Me Fly"
"Readjustment Blues"
"The Eagle and The Hawk"
"Tools"

Rocky Mountain High - *(RCA #LSP-4731).* 1972 (Fall)

"Rocky Mountain High"
"Mother Nature's Son"
"Paradise"
"For Baby (For Bobbie)"
"Darcy Farrow"
"Prisoners"
"Goodbye Again"
"Season Suite: Summer, Fall, Winter, Late Winter, Early Spring (When Everybody Goes to Mexico), Spring"

Farewell Andromeda - *(RCA #APL1-0101).* 1973 (Summer)

"I'd Rather Be a Cowboy"
"Berkeley Woman"
"Please, Daddy"
"Angels from Montgomery"
"River of Love"
"Rocky Mountain Suite (Cold Nights in Canada)"
"Whiskey Basin Blues"
"Sweet Misery"

"Zachary and Jennifer"
"We Don't Live Here No More"
"Farewell Andromeda (Welcome to My Morning)"

John Denver's Greatest Hits - *(RCA #CPL1-0374)* 1973 (Fall)

"Leaving, on a Jet Plane"
"Take Me Home, Country Roads"
"Poems, Prayers & Promises"
"Rocky Mountain High"
"For Baby (For Bobbie)"
"Starwood in Aspen"
"Rhymes & Reasons"
"Follow Me"
"Goodbye Again"
"The Eagle and the Hawk"
"Sunshine on My Shoulders"

Back Home Again - *(RCA #CPL1-0548)*. 1974

"Back Home Again"
"On the Road"
"Grandma's Feather Bed"
"Matthew"
"Thank God I'm a Country Boy"
"The Music Is You"
"Annie's Song"
"It's Up to You"
"Cool an' Green an' Shady"
"Eclipse"
"Sweet Surrender"
"This Old Guitar"

An Evening with John Denver - *(RCA #CPL2-0764)*. 1975

"The Music Is You"
"Farewell Andromeda (Welcome to My Morning)"
"Mother Nature's Son"
"Summer"
"Today"
"Saturday Night in Toledo, Ohio"
"Matthew"
"Rocky Mountain Suite (Cold Nights in Canada)"
"Sweet Surrender"
"Grandma's Feather Bed"
"Annie's Song"
"The Eagle and the Hawk"
"My Sweet Lady"
"Annie's Other Song"
"Boy from the Country"
"Rhymes & Reasons"
"Forest Lawn"
"Pickin' the Sun Down"
"Thank God I'm a Country Boy"
"Take Me Home, Country Roads"
"Poems, Prayers & Promises"
"Rocky Mountain High"
"This Old Guitar"

Windsong - *(RCA #APL1-1183)*. 1975 (Fall)

"Windsong"
"Cowboy's Delight"
"Spirit"
"Looking for Space"
"Shipmates and Cheyenne"
"Late Nite Radio"
"Love Is Everywhere"
"Two Shots"
"I'm Sorry"
"Calypso"
"Fly Away"
"Song of Wyoming"

Rocky Mountain Christmas - *(RCA #APL1-1201)* 1975 (Winter)

"Rudolph, the Red-Nosed Reindeer"
"Silver Bells"
"Silent Night"
"The Christmas Song"
"Christmas for Cowboys"
"Please, Daddy"
"Oh Holy Night"
"What Child Is This?"
"Coventry Carol"
"Away in a Manger"
"A Baby Just Like You"

The Spirit - *(RCA #APL1-1694)*. 1976 (Summer)

"Come And Let Me Look In Your Eyes"
"Eli's Song"
"Wrangle Mountain Song"
"Hitchhiker"
"In the Grand Way"
"Polka Dots and Moonbeams"
"It Makes Me Giggle"
"Baby, You Look Good To Me Tonight"
"Like A Sad Song"
"San Antonio Rose"
"Pegasus"
"The Wings That Fly Us Home"

read all about them

What's it like to be a superstar? Find out in these beautiful best-selling books—each containing *hundreds* of fantastic photos.

Paul McCartney: In His Own Words

A Conversation With Elton John

Joni Mitchell: Her Life, Her Loves, Her Music

Reflections of a Rock Star by Ian Hunter

Hendrix: Interviews With Those Closest to Jimi

Each is 7 by 10, $3.95 paperbound. Available at your local book and music stores or directly from: Quick Fox, Dept. RS 33 West 60th Street, New York 10023. Add 50¢ for postage and handling. Write for FREE catalog.